MICHAEL JACKSON

ON BLACK SPACE AND
BLACK BODIES: 1987-1997
A VIDEO ANALYSIS

A SHORT NOTE

ISBN : 978-1-63752-735-1

The 1980s, as many of us know, marked the last decade of the Cold War, the fall of the Berlin Wall in 1989 symbolizing the end of an era. Though the ex- Yougoslavia territories were still burning, as the consequences of proxy wars, most Western nations were turned toward the prospect of globalism, freedom and slowly began to reject the idea of nationalism and of the nation-state as a whole. As the war caused many casualties around the world, it is more than important to remember that the emphasis was put on the technological competition between the USSR and the United States and its West European allies.

Actually, the United States managed to become the giant of the former century due to the investments on technology and the Internet. Indeed, the politicians apprehended the future and led the world toward a global and homogenous power which would be dominated by the American force. One main support used by the United States was the expansion of television, the first global village, through which the world would be exposed to the American Dream and way of life. That would be synonym with freedom, creativity, multiculturalism and freedom of expression. The visual culture was always proper to the English speaking world. Indeed, as early as the beginning of the British colonial reign, images and photos were used as powerful means of propaganda to assert the dominant position of the Crown overseas. Though the French were the first ones interested in developing movie theaters, as illustrated by the Brothers Lumière, the United States would elevate the power of propaganda, along with the German Nazis as early as 1935. If Europe primarily focused on writing, the Americans used images to target and influence the behavior of a given people. Edward Bernays, a nephew of Sigmund Freud, would change the impact of the visuals in publicity with the release of his work, *Propaganda* in 1929, in which he wrote about the efficient consequences of the use of images in manipulating the masses and encourage them to consume even more. Images would speak a thousand words in a short amount of time. Therefore, the massive investments in movie companies were never a matter of chance but a real political move from the United States. Their domination had to be both technological -we must include the army too- and cultural. Strangely enough, though Black Americans were criminalised and the main victims of police brutality in the 1980s and 1990s, African-American singers would be the first to help America assert its domination worldwide without even knowing it. By the 80s, Western European societies began to change and evolve towards multiculturalism as many Africans, who had been colonised a few years prior, left their nations to migrate to Europe for economic or safety reasons. Most groups were isolated and were not represented in the media. Black American singers and actors would become the symbol for lost Black European groups who then felt represented and appreciated. The power of American music clearly came from the Black community as the members probably created all the genres played at the time, from rock, jazz, R'n'B, Rap to soul, or country influencing the world consequently. The United States allied the excellence of their artists to the endless forms of technological progress. Music labels and movie corporations were the key factors in the development of the American way of life. In this sense, Michael Jackson, played a very important role in the positive representation of the black body. A talented singer and incredible dancer, Jackson became the very first international global figure at the time, hence a Black man who found himself able to surpass any frontier, ethnic group, culture due to the extraordinary body of work he presented. He not only dominated and influenced, but he also, mostly, created the codes for modern day pop music. Strangely enough, Jackson did seem to have absorbed the American tactics as he, himself, used the progress of technology to further his worldwide impact. This work is a short political and cultural note which aims to reinterpret the impact of the black body in the visuals of Jackson from 1987 to 1997. It was designed to be this way.

THE LIBERATION OF THE BLACK BODY IN AN OPPRESSIVE ENVIRONEMENT : JAM

In 1992, Michael Jackson released the new single for the *Dangerous* project launched a year prior. Though a commercial success, *Jam* remains one of the most underrated songs in the Jackson catalogue. As the lyrics question the state of the world at the time and the human condition, the music video in itself, was one of the deepest social statements made by the singer. First of all, the video themes in the works of Michael Jackson often evolve around duality: good vs bad, authority vs freedom, wealth vs poverty, social groups/family vs individualism and light vs darkness. In *Jam*, the main aesthetics oppose destitution (or geographical decay) to beauty and confinement of the ghetto to freedom.

The video was shot in the projects of Chicago in an abandoned area characterised by the heavy destitution of the buildings and the ruins surrounding the environement. The ghetto was also heavily present in the extended video version of 1987 *Bad*. In *Jam*, the space could be separated into two specific sections: the abandoned building made to be a house where Jackson and Jordan perform and the outside. The exterior world is synonym with anger, dysfunction, danger and insecurity. This idea is reinforced by the beginning of the video. Before the song opens, the camera slowly focuses on a window from which a couple arguing can be heard before a basket ball is thrown outside, breaking the one of the principal windows. Yet, interestingly enough, in this destitute area, none of the windows from that building had been broken before the ball was thrown out. The broken window is a subtle meaning for the rupture in the family home but also in the Black community, especially for those who live in the ghetto. Michael Jackson and

Michael Jordan remain in the abandoned building/house and therefore provide the stability children can not find in their original homes and in the streets. Jackson would provide them with a shelter. This specific characteristic is also echoed in *Ghosts*, the short movie which would be launched in 1996 and another hymn for the isolated and excluded of society as we will see later on. It is in this decrepit house, though broken and in shacks, that the children find the essential. Indeed, there, they can enjoy the freedom of their minds by the expression of their bodies. The abandoned building represents the place of the isolated, those the good society does not want to see and embrace. Jackson clearly takes the place of the male caretaker, the big brother or even mother of a lost generation. The decaying and horrid color of the buildings is opposed to the beauty of the Black bodies present within the given space. Contrary to the shots of the outside world, the Black bodies are not dominated by a heavy and depressing environement as they manage to conduct the eyes of the TV watchers to the essential and the beauty of their characteristics. If not one single indication explains the history background behind the construction of the space and the ghetto the bodies live in, it is easy to imagine the causes of such dismay. By the time the video was released, in 1992, the Black community had been greatly plagued by the crack epidemic of the 1980s, a great economic recession and the AIDS crisis as well. Due to the tough Ronald Reagan laws which led to the massive incarceration of Black men, African-Americans were once again physically criminalised and made the main enemies of the United States. The specific ghetto of the video has no name but it is clear that the isolation is the consequence of such unfair policies led by the American government against the Black

Americans. Interestingly enough, outside of Jordan and Jackson, all the characters present in the video are children and teenagers. The adults are not present at all. This could signify that they failed. The argument at the beginning of the video does not allow us to see the faces of the protagonists fighting. Yet we recognise that they are adults. The danger of the environement plunged them into a state of ignorance of their own children who were playing outside. Obsessed with their financial and social problems, the adults failed the new generation by reproducing a vicious cycle and remained strangers to the stress, pain and sadness left in the soul of their own children. By playing in the streets, which resemble a battlefield after a huge bombing similar to that of Sarajevo, the video indicates that the children are left on their own by the families. The focus on the Black children and their bodies is symbolic in the sense that they are the spiritual wealth and the future of a nation. They would be the living plants growing out of a destitute and abandoned land. Children are supposed to embody the future and though made to never make out of the ghetto, they can elevate their minds and be exposed to the beauty of their own talents and gifts within the house occupied by Jackson and Jordan. Some are musicians, playing the trumpet, others dance, play basketball, sit by a window to think and simply exist. In the video, art frees the minds of these children, breaking the cycle of repetition, not being able to break the mental chains.

What about the relationship of the viewer to beauty and ugliness? Michael Jackson, through the body of the dancer, appears to be extremely confident in his movements and in his body. This fact is deeply highlighted by the simplicity of his clothes and the space he dances in. The destitution becomes beautiful and magic as soon as he starts to move. The control of the steps, which are proper to him, encourage us to forget the sad display of the decay and the unoccupied building. By using the deserted edifice as a simple stage, Jackson manages to cross the social and territorial spheres meant to be scary to the outside world, especially for the Whites living in the good areas. The ruins of the environement are also linked to the artistic state of the African-American community at the time and a testimony when it comes to the story of success and elevation within the music industry. Indeed, dance, music or sports are gifts Black Americans have always created, dominated and yet, such triumphs have been taken away from them too, leaving the original creators in a state of poverty, left to their own ruins as they were stolen. In the 1980s and 1990s, the Black Americans were exploited for their gifts yet criminalised and left outside of the spotlight. The political manipulation of that time led many to wrongly believe the emergence of Black American millionaires, in the 1980s, to be a great sign of prosperity for the whole community when it was never the case at all. The people in pain were simply kept hidden and in isolation.

The Power of Transmission

The power of transmission between generations is one important theme in the video as well. By paying closer attention, one realises that Jackson was always in the house/building. Yet, one specific shot shows Jordan walking towards the camera. This would mark a symbolic return of the basketball legend to his roots. Not only on a social level but as a community. Despite the fame of their status, both Jordan and Jackson convey a message to the media. If they appreciate and love their talents, the journalists can not dare to separate the men from their own community, whether in good or bad, the Black community they badly portray are their roots too. The ruins are also a symbol of equality. Though rich, famous and legendary in their respective fields, Jackson and Jordan started from nothing and worked endlessly to achieve their goals. In this sense, the lack of artifices in the edifice is a direct message to the youth, indicating that work would be the only value which would allow them to rise to the top. Such rhetoric was the expansion of the American Dream as well. The poverty and brokeness which characterise the space are not just geographical but are a testimony of a shattered legacy within the

Black community which would go back to the times of slavery and segregation. These two terrible events which followed each other would later give birth to a social destabilization distinguished by broken homes due to the trauma of deportation and split families by the White masters, racial and social exclusion, drug abuse, gang violence and torments. By excluding them, Black Americans became the ghosts of their own towns. The element that slavery and segregation affected even more was the power of transmission. This symbol is not only shown through the representation of the house where the children and the two

Michaels stay but through the ball thrown out of the window at the beginning. The ball is actually a world map. This detail refers to the freedom of expansion of the mind, a possible desire to explore the earth and move out of the ghetto, the talent and passion of a child which will not be spoiled or diminished, a hope for the next generations in the future of the Black community. In this sense, the presence of Jordan and Jackson would make great sense. The two men would return to the house to show the youth encouragement and pride in who they are and uplift them in not letting poverty break them for Jordan and Jackson succeeded in making out of their own difficulties to become legends. The house is the place of recognition where the two men give back to those who have always elevated them, the Black community. Out of the shacks, they hope to rebuild and make the first step. Before being artistic bodies, Jackson and Jordan are Black bodies who do not forget about their origins. Their success stories broke with the vilification of Blacks throughout history but also with the 1980s and 1990s gang violence and crime. By coming back to the original point they build a new chain which will hopefully grow and be fruitful. The depth of this message takes a visual form with the last shot of the video, as the last child picks up the ball thrown in the first seen. The basket ball which is also a world map as we said earlier is picked up from a puddle. The water is symbol of life, rebirth and rejuvenation. Both Jordan and Jackson pass the torch to their own, the younger generation. The globe possessed by the children is also echoed in the *Black or White* video in a particular scene where two babies sit on it.

By breaking the chains in their minds, and with the power of transmission, Black children can make it as long as they work harder to achieve their goals.

THE BLACK BODY CONQUEROR AND THE POWER OF REAPPROPRIATION: REMEMBER THE TIME AND BLACK OR WHITE

Global media did attempt to take away Michael Jackson from his Blackness and African heritage. By the 1980s, though a victim of racial discrimination by MTV, the White media want Jackson to be perceived as a colorless global icon and not a Black man. His tremendous talent needs to be shared and appropriated by the White establishment. Yet, as his appearence changed over the years, his message became

Blacker and more conscious. The real inventor of the art of videography, the Black bodies are always portrayed in the most powerful and positive ways in the imagery of Jackson. In the *Black or White* video, the singer replaces the Black body in its glory. After the White American patriarch has been brutally expelled from the roof of his house due to the heavy sound of the guitar- this scene being more of a fantasy rather than a real event which would have organically taken place-, the latter crashes in Africa, or what is supposed to be an African space. This would be the first shot as soon as the music plays.

Africa is the place of origin of the first man. Yet, this section is also specific to Jackson who centers and asserts his knowledge of self, as a Black man in America, in his desire to embrace his Black African blood and ethnicity. In the video, the men are almost naked, their skin painted and they wear traditional attires. Once again, Jackson opposes two aspects between nakedness and the idea of weakness. In this particular scene, the naked Black men dominate their environement, the savanna and this strength is embodied by the presence of the lions, (the kings of the jungle and symbol of virility in many African societies), they are chasing and trying to hunt. By this representation, Jackson breaks with the stereotypes surrounding Native Africans often portrayed in the American media as being poor, weak and unable to stand strong. Michael gives them their strength back. The nudity refers to the original state of man. Indeed, it is clear that all children were born naked. The bodies are thus freed from any religious or social stigmas, dogmas and judgments made by the Western world and their leaders who consider to be more advanced than the populations living in the southern hemisphere. Armed with lenses and arrows and ready to hunt the lions, the naked Black men then proceed to execute traditional African dance steps surrounding Jackson and still in their African space. They are the conquerors in their own space. The fact that the African dancers are shot in the very first section clearly refers to the fact that any other race on the planet finds its roots in Africa. The blend would also be reinforced by the famous morphing scene in the end. Yet, when it comes to the self-affirmation of his heritage, *Remember The Time* remains the most important testament in the career of Jackson. Over the years, he elevated his status and invested in his own work. In a global world where the emphasis

31

was put on the image, the video being used a modern propaganda and marketing tool, the importance of *Remember The Time* relies on the narrative. As a Black man, he controls it and gets to tell the story, reversing the place of Black Africans in the diaspora, in spheres exploited by Black bodies. *Remember The Time* breaks with the message of diversity promoted in the *Black or White* through which different races were introduced. This time around, the video does not include any other race at all. Not one single White body could be noticed, a fact which clearly indicates that Jackson was eager to change and replace the colonial whitewashed tale, by giving Black people their space of glory. The attachment of African-Americans to Africa at the time is the direct legacy inherited from the Black Panthers, the 60s movements and the emphasis put on Black consciousness. The inclusivity is reinforced by the closed space of the scenes. There is no way to enter for the outsiders and the space is theirs. In this glorious space, the beauty is emphasised on Black physical attributes: the diversity of the features, the physical strength and bodies but also Black women and their natural hair and braids. The video contracts with the colonial narrative concerning Ancient Egypt and

African spaces in history promoted by Hollywood. Black African Egyptians were excluded from the top position and were sent to remain in the back of the shot scenes. In *Remember The Time*, Black people are royalty and placed at the center of the narrative. Representation also matters in this given space. Indeed, the painting on the walls portray the Black individuals whom inhabit the court. This contributes to the creation of a certain harmony between the body and the Egyptian temple for the Black body, in the video, is the temple. The choreography serves this filming purpose. The dancers are one single body, and this unity is maintained by a the coordination of their moves. The men and women, hence the Black male and female energy, complete each other as one.

THE BODY IN ISOLATION: GHOSTS

A true underrated masterpiece, Michael showed how his dance moves and performances were even more sophisticated than before. Yet, if unfair critics considered the movie to be a second Thriller, *Ghosts* is actually a deep social statement made by the singer who definitely knows where he stands: among the outcasts. The story evolves around an isolated man, played by

Jackson- who lives in an abandoned and dirty manoir filled with entities deprived of speech, until they are disturbed by an abusive patriarch surrounded by kids and other family members and friends who hope to threaten Jackson's character. It is true that the problematic of the patriarch is extremely present in MJ's videos. In *Black or White*, *Ghosts* or many other videos made to be funny, the father is always an oppressive figure who prevents the children from becoming who they are. (This is a clear hint at the trauma experienced at the hands of Joe Jackson).

In the video, Jackson also plays a lot with *voyeurism* giving the audience the most horrific faces he can make. He distorts his eyes, his flesh, turns into a monster, a skeleton, alternates between phases of joy and anger, being threatening at times, and even breaks his face against the tiled floor.

The short movie asks us one question. Who are the monsters? And why are the monsters ghosts? Are they invisible spiritual entities Jackson can make appear out of nowhere, or do these creatures hide voluntarily to stay away from individuals who have constantly shamed and rejected them for being different or living in the norm? The castle is isolated and the mere existence of such abnormal individual threatens the peace of the good society. The appearence of the monsters reveal that society is responsible for the demise of the outcasts. Society condemns, attacks and rejects those who can not fit in. One specific symbol in the movie is how the hosts alternate between period of fear, angst and admiration watching the dancers and Jackson execute the most elaborate dance moves before their eyes. This conveys the message that society only likes to exploit the creativy of the isolated. Their pain and rejection give them a sense of authenticity the norm is deprived of. In reality, the outcasts are the ones who can truly change the norm for they are filled with the strength of their unique vision. The rise of flamenco in Spain could be one example. Created by Africans, Gypsies, Jews, Arabs and Andalusians, the genre now stands as the official symbol of Spanish identity. Yet, the originators are still exluded from enjoying the results of their creation as they remain discriminated. Society creates its own monsters and the reclusion experienced by the entities in the movie embody the consequences of such isolation. Though portrayed as monsters or ghosts,

the creatures also constitute the Black
bodies, not on a racial level, but socially.
They would be the ones living in the danger
zone good people would fear to fall into. The
constant disdain and contempt imposed
upon the individuals who do not correspond
to the perfect social vision of the Western
sphere nurtures low self-esteem, abusive
behaviors and somehow leads to the
emergence of serial killers. If some of them
were deeply evil since the beginning and
had no regrets in the pain they inflicted
onto others, the majority has been pushed
to the edge by the good members of society
who turned a blind eye, ridiculed them and

had few consideration for their inability to follow a perfect scheme. A serial killer or marginalized individual carry, for the most part, a certain attitude which is never represented as the norm. Such difference would be another factor to justify their execution or condemnation. We judge the final products, the brutal actions, consequences, yet, society would never take any responsability for the roots of the problem. Sending a troubled woman who was failed by society her entire life to the electric chair would be easier than facing the real mistakes and failures of the system we created.

Ghosts allows us to wonder who are the monsters? Are these people dancing with Michael and deprived of speech really repulsive or does society and its biased ideas of the norm did condition our brains and minds to believe such things and to condemn those who are different from the perfect? It is true for Michael that the media, the judgements of others led him to the self-hatred of his self and deep sad mental issues which would have plagued him for the rest of his life until 2009. Life in the Western sphere, especially under the capitalistic reign, not only forces us to deny the existence of those who failed to enter such oppressive system, but worst, we deny and suppress any traits within us which would link us to the outsiders. For this reason, depressed women and men, unhappy with their jobs, careers, who married and began a life to please their parents would rather cheat on their spouse, take antidepressant pills or do drugs to evade and suppress the unknown within them, fearing the ultimate explosion could send them live to the other side, where the ghosts and monsters live. The Western sphere is sick yet, the technological developments and our ability to show a false good life on social media give us a superficial satisfaction of success all the while comparing ourselves to others. The freaks and rejected are abandoned yet they ignore everything about their own power. They are not loved or embraced yet they enjoy a good amount of freedom, hence a strength the good citizen would never experience. *Ghosts* by MJ is a good social symbol of it. Made in 1997, it embodies the decay of the society we live in, the pain judgement inflict and the strong desire of the isolated to stand up and fight against the dominant and corrupted.

www.ingramcontent.com/pod-product-compliance
Lightning Source LLC
Chambersburg PA
CBHW061520180526
45171CB00001B/269